Big Annie

D0521282

MVFOL

Also by Jerry Stanley:

CHILDREN OF THE DUST BOWL
The True Story of the School at Weedpatch Camp

I AM AN AMERICAN
A True Story of Japanese Internment

Big Annie
of Calumet

A True Story
of the
Industrial Revolution

by Jerry Stanley

illustrated with photographs

HAMPTON-BROWN

To Annie Clemenc

and the women of Calumet

Hampton-Brown
P.O. Box 223220
Carmel, CA 93922
1-800-333-3510

Printed in the United States of America.

Map art by Karen McKee

Picture Credits can be found following the index.

Library of Congress Cataloging-in-Publication Data
Stanley, Jerry, 1941-
Big Annie of Calumet: a true story of the industrial Revolution / by Jerry Stanley.
—1st ed.
p. cm.
Includes bibliographical references and index.
Summary: The story of Annie Clemenc and the 1913 strike by copper miners
employed by the Calumet & Hecla Mining Company in Upper Michigan.
1. Clemenc, Ana K., 1888-1956—Juvenile literature. 2. Women labor leaders—
Michigan—Biography—Juvenile literature. 3. Labor movement—Michigan—History—
20th century—Juvenile literature. 4. Copper Miners' Strike, Mich., 1913-1914—Juvenile
literature. 5. Strikes and lockouts—Copper mining—Michigan—History—20th
century—Juvenile literature. [1. Clemenc, Annie. 2. Labor leaders. 3.
Women—Biography. 4. Copper Miners' Strike, Mich., 1913-1914. 5. Strikes and
lockouts.] I. Title.
HD8073.C55S83 1995
331.89'2822343'092—dc20
[B] 95-18856
ISBN 0-7362-1244-2

05 06 07 08 09 10 10 9 8 7 6 5 4 3

Contents

Introduction: Big Annie

Annie Clemenc was twenty-five years old when she marched down a muddy road carrying an American flag and tried to change her life. For her mother and father, brothers and sisters, and for her husband and herself, life in Upper Michigan was difficult and the future looked bleak. Hard work was no guarantee that there would be enough food on the table or money left over to buy shoes, coats, and bedding. The men in her family worked in mines deep underground—for six days a week, eleven hours a day—and earned $2.50 a day each. If Annie was lucky, she could earn fifty cents a day scrubbing floors and washing other people's clothing.

She had grown up in a shack and still lived in a shack. She had grown up wearing dresses bought in secondhand stores and still wore dresses bought in secondhand stores. She wanted to have children and raise a family of her own—but not if they had to live in poverty. She could spend the rest of her life scrubbing floors and getting nowhere, or she could try to get out of poverty by marching against the people who kept her in poverty. In the summer of 1913, she decided to march.

Annie lived at a time when workers had few legal rights to organize and try to get higher wages. Business owners determined the wages workers would be paid, the length of the workday, and the conditions at work. Too often these wages weren't enough to live on, and the work environment was dangerous. Every day when her husband and her father went to work in the mines, Annie feared that they might be killed or crippled for life in a cave-in.

In her desire to improve the lives of workers and make a future for her own children, she discovered that being patient, silent, and ladylike wasn't the answer—but that maybe bold action was. When she decided to defy 3,000 armed men and an entire state militia, she chose as her symbol of determination a large American flag, too large for most men to carry for ten miles a day, as she did. She marched and the men followed, and when her opponents tried to stop her, she dipped a broom in human waste and beat them on the head. When they knocked her down and cut her flag to pieces with swords, she got up and kept marching, saying she would rather die than give in. She was a heroine to 9,000 men, women, and children, and her story is the story of the people who built America and made it the richest and most powerful nation on earth.

1   The Industrial Revolution

The workers who followed Annie were participants in one of the greatest events in American history, the Industrial Revolution. It occurred between 1860 and 1920, when 33 million immigrants from all parts of the world came to America seeking opportunity and a better life. Most were poor and couldn't afford to buy farmland or start a business. But they had the muscle needed to build an industrial empire, and they were not afraid of hard work.

They were known as the "new immigrants." Prior to 1860, most of the immigrants to America came from northern and central Europe, many from England. The new immigrants came from southern and eastern Europe—from Italy, Russia, Poland, Croatia, and Greece. Unlike the immigrants from northern Europe, who were Protestant and spoke English, the new arrivals were Catholic, Greek Orthodox, and Jewish, and the multitude of languages and customs they brought with them gave America a rich tradition of ethnic and cultural diversity. In 1860, southern and eastern Europeans made up only 1 percent of the foreign-born population in America, but by 1910 they

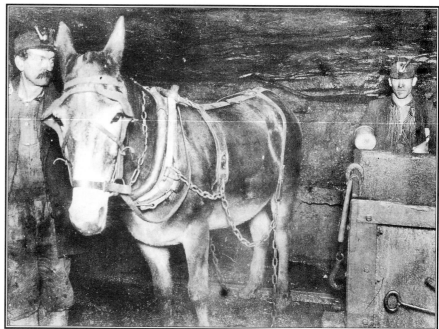

Scenes from the American industrial revolution:

(Top left) Railroad construction, second half of the nineteenth century.

(Top right) Steelworkers in Homestead, Pennsylvania, about 1890.

(Right) Coal miners, late nineteenth century.

(Facing page, top) Women workers in a textile factory, about 1890.

(Facing page, bottom) A machine shop, operated by the General Electric Company, about 1895.

made up 38 percent of the foreign-born population. Between 1860 and 1920, the population of the United States tripled as a result of the new immigrants, and this migration was the largest movement of people in history.

Before 1860, American industries were still producing for a

farm economy: a pair of tongs for a blacksmith in Vermont, a plow for a farmer in New York. The American Civil War, which was fought from 1861 to 1865, stimulated industrial development: swords, bullets, cannons, and fighting ships were all needed to wage that mighty battle. With the arrival of the new immigrants and the outbreak of the Civil War, all the elements were in place for the start of the Industrial Revolution.

Railroads led the way with the construction of the transcontinental railroad between 1862 and 1869. As branch lines were built out from the railroad, more steel and different fuels were needed. Industries arose to make new metals, to process foods, and to mass-produce shirts, dresses, hats, and shoes for an ever-increasing population. Croats, Czechs, Greeks, and Poles scrambled to the steel mills of Pennsylvania, the coal mines of West Virginia, the stockyards of Chicago, and the copper range of Michigan's Upper Peninsula. Others crowded into cities: Jews in the garment trade, Lithuanians and Portuguese in the textile towns of New England. In 1907, 15,858 of the 23,337 workers at the Carnegie steelworks were foreign-born. In 1909, 76 percent of the workers in the coal mines of Pennsylvania were of foreign birth, and 92 percent of those came from southern and eastern Europe.

One new industry triggered the birth of another—fuel for locomotives, ships for hauling iron ore, new machinery for making gears, rails, cotter pins, and presses. Few could keep track of the staggering statistics in the economic revolution or calculate its significance. Yet one thing was clear: In 1860, the United States was a debtor nation whose industry was primarily agricultural; in 1920, it was the leading manufacturing power in the world, with more than 9 million industrial workers producing goods valued at $62 billion.

During the Industrial Revolution, a small group of men gained control of the natural resources in America. Aided by the federal government, which gave them loans and grants of natural resources, or sold the resources for a fraction of their value, these men organized huge corporations that controlled a certain raw material needed to produce a certain product; iron ore for making steel, timber for building ships, coal for fuel, copper for the manufacture of electric wire. As these corporations grew, they drove out smaller businesses and gained control of more raw materials. In 1880 alone, 115 railroad companies were swallowed up by the larger railroad corporations, and by 1879 John D. Rockefeller's Standard Oil Corporation controlled 90 percent of the nation's oil-refining capacity. Rockefeller's corporation, like the other companies that controlled 70 percent or more of an important raw material, was called a "monopoly" because it was big enough to drive out competitors.

The monopolies produced tremendous profits for the men who ran them. Before the Civil War there were almost no millionaires, but by 1892 there were 4,047, almost all in industry. The four men who ran the Central Pacific Railroad Corporation made a profit of $200 million. The railroad baron Cornelius Vanderbilt was worth $200 million, the steel tycoon Andrew Carnegie $250 million, and Rockefeller $900 million.

The giant companies that controlled mining or manufacturing properties also controlled whole towns where their businesses were located. Textile firms in the South owned entire counties—all the streets, houses, stores, schools, churches, and utilities—and ran the local police. In the mining communities of Colorado, Kentucky, and Pennsylvania, and in the lumber towns of the West, corporations controlled most aspects of life. In 1914, even a United States congressman had to secure a pass to enter one of the towns owned by the Colorado Fuel and Iron Company.

To increase productivity, the corporations developed new

machinery, making workers adapt to the machines instead of adapting the machines to the workers. The goal was increased profits, little of which were to be passed on to workers in the form of higher wages or a shorter workday. Many companies cared for the welfare of their workers and paid them a fair wage—for example, the auto builder Henry Ford paid his workers five dollars a day and was mindful that the workplace was safe. But others refused to share even one cent of increased profits. As one of them said, "We are the rich; we own America; we got it, God knows how, but we intend to keep it."

The result for many workers was something less than what they had sought when they came to America. Performing the backbreaking labor that made possible the Industrial Revolution, vast numbers of the new immigrants worked for poverty wages in dirty and unsafe conditions. Of all the industrial nations in the world, the United States had the highest accident and death rate for workers. For all industries, it has been estimated that at the turn of the century there were 35,000 deaths and more than 2 million serious injuries from accidents on the job *each year*—a daily toll of 112 dead and 6,389 injured. By the turn of the century most European nations had workmen's compensation laws for injuries on the job, but the United States did not.

Other nations also had laws setting a minimum wage and limiting the number of hours in a workday, but again the United States did not. In 1900, 70 percent of industrial workers worked at least ten hours a day. As late as 1923, the steel industry had a twelve-hour workday and a seven-day workweek. Whether a miner or a factory worker, an unskilled laborer earned less than ten dollars a week, while the pay for women

(Facing page) This woman was widowed and her seven children were left fatherless when a coal mining accident in Wilkes-Barre, Pennsylvania, in 1919 killed her husband and ninety-two others.

and children, who made up well over half of the work force, averaged five dollars a week—for a twelve-hour day and a seven-day week! From 1880 to 1910, the average annual family income of industrial workers was $525.27. With living expenses averaging $507.56, there was less than twenty dollars a year left over to make life more pleasurable and fun.

Statistics alone do not convey the poverty and shattered dreams of the workers. Most had become naturalized citizens, and their children were American citizens by birth. They

Young boys working as miners in the Pennsylvania coal fields, about 1895. Child labor laws had not yet been enacted to protect children.

believed in America as a land of opportunity for all, but found that their only reward for hard work was the misery of poverty and the fear of injury and death. Not surprisingly, they searched for a way to improve their lives: "When a man is steady and sober," one of them said, "and . . . finds himself in debt for a common living, something must be wrong."

When they asked their employers for better wages and work conditions, they collided with all the might and arrogance of a business system where workers had few, if any, rights. There

was a disregard for workers as human beings in the comment of one manufacturer: "I regard my employees as I do a machine, to be used to my advantage, and when they are old and of no further use, I cast them into the street." There was cruelty in the comment of railroad tycoon Cornelius Vanderbilt: "Law! What do I care about law? Hain't I got the power?" There was down-right meanness in the remark of millionaire Jay Gould: "I can hire one half of the working class to kill the other half."

The workers responded to this hostile attitude by going on strike. In 1874, Pennsylvania coal miners struck for a higher wage. Their employers imported outside workers and starved the miners into submission. In 1877, new wage cuts added a final straw to the grievances of railroad workers. Their strike was ended by federal troops. A 1903 strike by coal miners at Cripple Creek, Colorado, was crushed when the governor declared martial law and rushed in state troops. The military commander arrested workers without charging them, destroyed miners' camps, locked miners up in bullpens, and seized food sent in for relief.

Women also struck during the Industrial Revolution. In 1909, garment workers in New York walked off the job when their wages were cut and their hours increased. "We are starving while we work," one woman said. "We may as well starve while we strike." Groups of 15,000 women marched in parades for months while donations of food kept their families alive. In 1912, women struck the textile mills in Lawrence, Massachusetts. One hundred women were attacked by 200 policemen, who beat the women to the ground with clubs.

The strikers won some concessions from their employers, but rarely what they had hoped for. The giant corporations had the

A confrontation between militia and men striking the Lawrence, Massachusetts, textile mills in 1912. Many of the participants in this strike were women.

wealth and power to fight a strike for months, import strike-breakers, hire detectives, carry the battle to court with highly paid lawyers, influence politicians, and, if necessary, shut down plants completely to force workers into submission.

Throughout the Industrial Revolution there was a double standard, one for business and one for workers. When corporations pooled their money to control an entire industry, it was considered a skillful business move; when workers tried to combine their numbers in a union, it was considered a conspiracy. The government helped corporations with gifts of land and natural resources, but government aid to workers was viewed as socialism. The use of the state militia to protect property was done to preserve law and order, but it was unthinkable to call in troops to support the cause of workers. To lay off workers and cut their pay was sound business practice, but to strike for better working conditions was to engage in extremism.

As much as anything else, this double standard was the root cause of the workers' poverty. As much as anything else, it caused Annie Clemenc to insist that workers have an equal right to organize and improve their lives. Like other children of immigrants, she believed that hard work should be rewarded with a fair wage and a safe workplace. Also like the others, she believed that she should have a say in her own life—and that the only way to get it was to demand it. Her story was once major news throughout much of America, and it took place on a frozen strip of land in the farthest reaches of the United States.

2   Keweenaw

The Keweenaw Peninsula in Northern Michigan is an icy finger of land that slices into the cold waters of Lake Superior. Described in 1844 as "a miserable, barren place," it consisted of densely timbered forests and forbidding swamps that bred swarming colonies of mosquitoes and flies. Stiff winds battered the peninsula nearly every day, and its winter lasted from September until April, when it was buried under an average snowfall of fifteen feet. There were no roads, no towns, and no people in the Keweenaw, except for a few fur traders and the Ojibwa Indians.

In 1845, huge deposits of copper were discovered in the peninsula, triggering the first major mining boom in the United States, four years before the more famous California gold rush of 1849. Previously, mining companies had focused on discovering veins of copper above ground that could be easily mined. It was a civil engineer named Edwin Hulbert who first explored the possibility of extracting copper from rock buried deep in the earth. Hulbert had poked around Michigan's Upper Peninsula for years, searching for the copper that was rumored to be there.

The Great Lakes

Copper Country

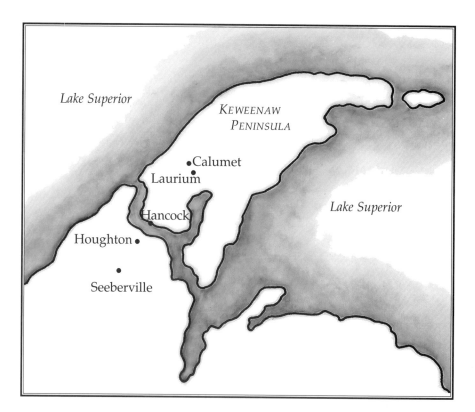

In 1845, he found it—by following some runaway pigs, legend says. Apparently he was chasing the pigs when they led him to an exposed vein of copper that extended for nearly a mile straight into the earth.

From 1845 to 1885, the Keweenaw Peninsula, now called Copper Country, became America's chief supplier of copper, mining half the copper in the United States—about 5 million tons a year. Propelled by the Civil War and the need for bronze cannons, the district experienced a boom as the price of copper rose from nineteen cents a pound in 1861 to fifty-five cents in 1864. By 1900, there were a dozen companies operating in Copper Country, led by the Boston-based Calumet and Hecla Mining Company. The C & H, as it was known, was the largest producer of copper and employed more than 7,000 men, more than half of the total work force of the peninsula. Between 1869 and 1913, C & H paid to its stockholders dividends of $150 million. The C & H mines were the richest copper mines in America, and their owners, Quincy Adams Shaw and Alexander Agassiz, used some of their profits to build Harvard University and fund the Boston Symphony Orchestra. Less than 5 percent of C & H's stock was owned by residents of the peninsula.

The earliest miners in Copper Country were single men who worked under extremely harsh conditions. To begin a mine, they made a clearing in the forest large enough for a bunkhouse, a blacksmith shop, a sawmill, and the engine and shaft houses. All their supplies were shipped by water from Detroit to the portage at Sault Sainte Marie. From here they were transshipped to the peninsula and unloaded onshore for the final leg of the journey, which took place on the miner's

(Left) An illustration depicts the crude tools used by the first miners to enter Copper Country.

(Right) A rare photograph of early copper miners using hand tools to extract ore.

back. Each miner carried a heavy barrel of salt pork and flour, lugging the cargo and other supplies along an Indian trail to the site of the mine.

Three men with a hand drill started a shaft, one man holding the large iron spike with both hands and the other two striking it with steel hammers. The hammering continued day and night as each three-member crew worked approximately eleven hours using a single drill and blasting powder to loosen the solid rock. By this crude method the men could sink up to 150 feet a year while other miners drilled "drifts"—branch tunnels at every 100-foot level leading out horizontally from the shaft in opposite directions, one to the left and one to the right. Some drifts were a quarter-mile long and were tunneled underneath Lake Superior within a hundred feet of its bottom. As the shaft

By the late nineteenth century, mining technology had progressed beyond hand tools. This drawing from the 1880s shows vertical "shafts," horizontal "drifts," and the new steam-powered drill in use. Also shown is the "kibble," an iron bucket used to haul ore to the surface.

A photo showing the steam-powered drills introduced to Copper Country in the 1880s.

was sunk deeper, ladders were used to enter and exit the mine, and often it took an hour to climb to the surface after working an eleven-hour shift. Many of the mines in the peninsula were the deepest in the world, one vertical mile.

Once loosened, the copper rock was transported from the drifts to the main shaft by wheelbarrows rolled along boards. The copper was hauled to the surface in a large iron bucket called a "kibble," which was attached to a heavy chain and powered by horses or men. From here it was hauled to a mill for stamping: crushing the rock, washing off debris, and salvaging the most copper possible. The copper was used for making a wide range of products, from electric wire to pots and pans and money.

In the 1880s, steam-powered air drills were introduced. They were operated by two men and could strike 380 blows a minute. Wheelbarrows were replaced by iron rail cars that hauled the rock from the drifts to the shaft, and the kibble was replaced by steam-powered cars that hauled the rock to the surface.

The opening of the Soo Canals between lakes Huron and Superior in 1855 caused shipping rates to drop and profits to soar for the C & H Mining Company, and the Keweenaw Peninsula was transformed into a series of thriving communities. By the turn of the century, Copper Country boasted three well-established cities: Houghton, Hancock, and the grand jewel of the peninsula, Calumet.

Calumet had a population of 33,000, but, unlike other communities of similar size, it was totally electrified and serviced by streetcars that ran twenty-four hours a day. All of its streets were paved, and telephones, still rare in much of the country, were commonplace. Calumet had more churches per capita than any other city in America, and its stores offered the finest wines, furs, and jewelry for those who could afford them: company officers of the C & H, bankers, doctors, and the like. In addition, the town had an ornate, three-story opera house, which became one of the nation's most renowned. Along with New York, Chicago, St. Louis, and San Francisco, Calumet was on the big-time entertainment circuit and featured leading performers such as Enrico Caruso, Douglas Fairbanks, Lillian Russell, and Sarah Bernhardt.

The two settlements that formed Calumet, Red Jacket and Laurium, were populated by immigrants from Europe who had come to America seeking a better life for themselves and their families. The Cornish from England were the first to arrive, bringing with them the experience of generations of miners. They were followed by Irishmen, Croats, Finns, Swedes, Italians, Hungarians, Poles, Austrians, Germans, Greeks, Armenians, Turks, Russians, and Chinese. By 1910 nearly 100,000 people lived in Copper Country, and 90 percent of them were of foreign descent. More than thirty different languages were spoken in Copper Country. Calumet had eight daily for-

Calumet: Fifth Street during winter.

The town of Calumet, with miners' homes in the foreground.

eign-language newspapers, and it was said that a miner could walk down the crowded streets of the town on a Saturday night and never hear English spoken.

The Calumet and Hecla Mining Company used some of its money to build Calumet. It built bathhouses, parks, a library, and a hospital. It rented out property for stores, churches, and schools. The company provided residents with free Lake Superior water, and it leased houses to its employees for six dollars a month, which was inexpensive.

But Calumet was a "company town." C & H owned the mines, the buildings, and the land under the buildings, which had been purchased from the federal government and the state of Michigan for perhaps 10 percent of the land's real value. C & H owned the streetcars and the opera house, the streets and the electricity, the trees, and even the grass, and C & H did with its holdings as it saw fit. When times were good, C & H was good to Calumet. When times were not so good, C & H was free to act in its own interest.

3 The Widow-Maker

By 1913, the Calumet and Hecla Mining Company was experiencing a decline in profits. The average mine depth was 4,000 feet, double what it had been just three decades earlier. In 1874, C & H had refined almost ninety-seven pounds of copper from every ton of ore. By 1913, that figure had dropped to just twenty-five pounds. C & H was having to dig deeper to get less.

To increase productivity, in 1913 the company ordered its workers to switch from the two-man drill to a one-man drill. The two-man drill had been in use for thirty years, and it allowed a worker to watch out for his partner in case of a cave-in or some other accident. Under the new plan, a 150-pound drill was mounted on a heavy iron post and operated by one man. If the post was struck by debris or collapsed from any cause, the miner was doomed, as the nearest man was 500 feet away. Miners called the new tool "the widow-maker" and feared having to use it.

Some of those who did, miner Paddy Dunnigan said from his own experience, were found "unconscious with their heads caved in." All the miners had to do was read almost any edition

A miner works alone with a steam-powered drill. Miners called the one-man-operated drill the "widow-maker."

of the *Calumet News* to see the widow-maker at work: July 2, 1913, "Solomon Kivisto was working on the 37th level when a fall of rock pinned him to the ground, breaking his neck"; July 5, "Martin Connors, age 30, died when he suffered a fractured skull as a result of a fall of loose ground in the Hecla branch of C & H"; July 16, "Dominic Massucco, age fifty, was working on the fortieth level when falling rock crushed his spine . . . He left a wife and seven children."

Besides the widow-maker, the miners had other grievances against C & H that they had been trying to remedy for years. Many had started working in the mines at the age of twelve, yet after thirty years of labor they had little to show for it. They worked in temperatures that ranged from 115 degrees to minus 27 degrees. They had no toilets, no water, and no food except what they brought themselves, and every day they faced rats "too big for a cat to tackle." Hammering away in the drifts for eleven hours a day, they were forced to breathe suffocating gas and smoke, and every day they faced the possibility of an accident or death—for which C & H assumed no responsibility. The company considered accidents and death "known risks" that workers freely assumed.

If workers refused to operate the one-man drill, they could be fired. If they asked for a raise or a shorter workday, they could be fired. Already, between 1907 and 1913, 3,000 miners quit C & H because of the bad conditions in the mines and the company's refusal to listen to workers. Said one miner, "In all these years that I have been working for this company we have been treated more and more like slaves. . . . The company drives us about like mules."

C & H believed it had little to fear from the workers in 1913, because the various ethnic groups working in the mines hated one another almost as much as they hated the company. The "Cousin Jacks," the Cornish, were the traditional enemies of the "Micks," the Irish, and they engaged in endless feuding throughout Copper Country. Once, when the outnumbered Irish fled to the second story of a saloon, the Cornishmen set it on fire. The Greeks hated the Turks, the Serbs and Croats didn't get along, and the Finns, plus most other groups, despised their Cornish foremen as company "stoolies." Each group had its own church—built on land owned by C & H—and of the ninety-nine saloons in Calumet—built on land owned by

C & H mine and shaft house at Calumet, around the turn of the century.

C & H—it was a brave man who ventured into the watering spot of another group.

Nevertheless, by 1913 the different groups had achieved some degree of unity, as they all had one thing in common: C & H's control over their lives. The traditional meal of the Cornish miner, the "pasty"—beef, potatoes, and onion baked in a turnover crust—was adopted by most other groups and came to symbolize Calumet. Parades to celebrate a holiday of one

group were joined by other groups, and all proudly marched in the Fourth of July and Christmas parades while still maintaining their separate identities. But more than anything else, the one-man drill helped the groups unite and operate collectively through a union—the Western Federation of Miners (WFM).

Labor unions had begun forming in the United States at the time of the Civil War. By 1864, blacksmiths, stonecutters, cigar makers, and carpenters had organized national unions, and by

1873 there were thirty-two such "nationals" representing about 300,000 workers. Because the unions represented skilled workers who were hard to replace, many companies recognized them and negotiated with them over wages and working conditions. This was not the case with factory workers or miners, who could easily be replaced and were easily replaced when they joined a union or went on strike. When miners struck C & H for higher wages in 1872, the company declared them "the most vicious and the most useless men we have in our employ." After three weeks of striking, the miners had spent their savings, their families were out of food, and the men returned to work. Although they won a small increase in wages, C & H refused to meet with representatives of the miners—even though they hadn't joined any union and weren't asking for union recognition.

Organized in 1893, the Western Federation of Miners won higher wages and a shortened workday for copper miners in Montana, Idaho, and Colorado. It was successful in gaining a four-dollar-a-day wage for eight and a half hours because so many miners had joined the union that they couldn't be quickly replaced. The WFM was also successful because it had funds to support a strike for months, as long as the work force wasn't too large. From 1908 to 1910, the WFM organized five local unions in Copper Country, and by 1913 more than 9,000 workers had joined it to challenge the power of C & H.

At the same time, the women of Copper Country had their own grievances against C & H, and they were also busy organizing to challenge the company. Always living on the edge of poverty, they spent endless hours caring for home and children while their fathers, husbands, and sons worked from sunup to sundown for a few dollars a day. To make ends meet, they planted small gardens, shopped at secondhand stores, and hired out as cooks, maids, and washerwomen, but they never got ahead. Many had seen their mothers endure the same struggle for thirty years and get nowhere, and the future for their own children looked grim. Living in constant fear of injury and death to their providers, in houses owned by C & H, in a town owned by C & H, the women of Calumet demanded that they have a say in their own lives.

Accordingly, in February 1913, the women of Hancock organized their own union: the Western Federation of Miners Auxiliary No. 5, to improve conditions in the mines and also to help unite the various ethnic groups by sponsoring dances and other social activities. Calumet women formed Auxiliary No. 15, Keweenaw women Auxiliary No. 16. In the summer of 1913, these women told their husbands that they should take no more and demand a return to the two-man drill. They would not be made widows at the hands of C & H, at least not without a fight. One of the women was Annie Clemenc, who had spearheaded the drive to organize Calumet's Auxiliary No. 15.

Annie was born in Calumet in 1888, the oldest of five children in her family. Her parents, George and Mary Klobuchar, were immigrants from Croatia, and her father raised the family by working in the C & H mines for thirty years while Mary worked as a cook and maid for the well-to-do. Annie graduated from a C & H school, became a church worker providing aid to crippled miners, and helped the family by taking in laundry.

At the age of eighteen Annie married Joseph Clemenc (pronounced "Clements"), a Croatian miner who was never mentioned in the numerous press accounts of his wife's activities.

She never mentioned him either. The only description of Joseph came from Annie's brother Frank, who said that Joseph was "quiet and mild-mannered" at six feet four inches tall. Annie was six feet two inches tall and just the opposite of quiet and mild-mannered.

Growing up, Annie had seen her mother and father work a lifetime for little more than clothing and enough food to get by. Her sisters wore hand-me-down dresses to school while her brothers entered the mines to start the same cycle of poverty for their families. On average, one worker a week died in the mines, and two were crippled for life every day. For most of her teenage years as a social worker, Annie had seen the crushed limbs and twisted bodies up close—and now came the widow-maker.

C & H miners gathered in front of the Calumet Miners' Union office. One sign mentions James McNaughton by name; another shows the one-man drill.

As a woman who wanted a life better than her mother's, Annie, quite simply, said no more. If her husband chose to be passive in the miners' activities, Annie chose otherwise. If Joseph thought it proper that his wife stay at home, Annie thought otherwise. This was her chance for a better life, and the time for ladylike was over. By the summer of 1913, Annie was ready for some action.

In the summer of 1913, the miners, at the urging of their wives and daughters, asked for a meeting with the mine owners to discuss three requests: a pay raise from $2.50 to $3.50 a day, a shorter workday, and a return to the two-man drill. From the miners' point of view, they were not asking for much—a modest improvement in their daily life. But from the mine owners' point of view, any recognition of a workers' union and any concession to such a union, however small, was unthinkable. The owners refused to recognize the miners' union and said no to any meeting; some of the miners' letters were returned unopened and marked REFUSED.

The national Western Federation of Miners was aware of events in Copper Country, and it advised against a strike; at the time the union's funds were too low to support 9,000 men and their families in a strike against C & H, the most powerful of all the copper companies. Disregarding the advice of the national union, on July 23, 1913, 9,000 miners out of a work force of 13,000 voted to go on strike. The reaction of the owners was swift. Their leader was James McNaughton, the $85,000-a-year general manager of C & H who lived in Calumet and directed the company's operations. He said, "The grass will grow on your streets before I'll ever give in." He added that he would teach the miners to eat potato parings.

C & H general manager James McNaughton, who told the miners "the grass will grow on your streets" before he would give in to their demands.

On the first day of the strike, through showers and a strong wind blowing off Lake Superior, some 500 striking miners marched down Calumet Avenue in perfect order to the C & H mines that bordered Red Jacket. But when they arrived, the orderly procession turned into an angry mob, as years of resentment toward C & H exploded. Picking up rocks, sticks, iron bolts, and four-foot gas pipes lying on the ground, the men swarmed over the property and clubbed C & H officials, driving them out of the mine buildings. At the end of the two-hour siege, the mines at Red Jacket were shut down.

On the second day of the strike, most of the mines in Houghton and Hancock were shut down, and miners were marching down the towns' main streets in mass demonstrations of unity. On the third day of the strike, 400 miners marched four abreast down Calumet Avenue for a rally; around the edge of the parade their wives and children stood holding hands in a show of support. Wearing a plain gingham house-dress, Annie Clemenc hoisted a massive American flag on a ten-foot staff, stepped to the front of the procession, and led the march. The other wives and children joined her in a show of determination. It was a scene that would torment the Calumet and Hecla Mining Company like a bad nightmare. Every day for the duration of the strike, Big Annie hoisted her flag and led the strikers in a show of relentless defiance. The fight was on.

Annie Clemenc, known as "Big Annie."

4 The Western Federation of Miners Must Go!

As many as 2,000 Finns, Croats, Hungarians, and Poles marched behind Big Annie for five to seven miles through the streets to the mines. The parades, held seven days a week starting at 6:00 A.M., became a symbol of the miners' unity, and Annie came to symbolize the determination of the women. The parades were also the most effective device the miners had for winning the strike, so long as they marched every day and did not let up. Timing their demonstrations to coincide with the hour that nonstriking miners went to work, the strikers, in an effort to shut down all the mines completely, urged the workers not to go. On Sundays, when workers had the day off, Annie led the women and children down Calumet Avenue wearing her white "Sunday best" dress trimmed with colorful ribbons. Two colored streamers ran down from the top of her flagstaff, the ends held by two little girls in white dresses.

Shocked at the defiance of the miners, C & H began marshaling its forces to meet the opposition. Scores of telegrams

The women, dressed in their "Sunday best," joined their husbands in the strike parades in a show of unwavering support.

began arriving in the state capital at Lansing, hundreds of miles to the south. Most were from shopkeepers and businessmen who owed their livelihood to C & H. Claiming that the region had been taken over by anarchists, the telegrams pleaded for state help. At James McNaughton's urging, Houghton County sheriff James Cruse wired the state capital: SITUATION HERE HAS BECOME DESPERATE. IMMEDIATE ACTION ON YOUR PART IS THE ONLY THING THAT WILL PREVENT GREATER DESTRUCTION OF PROPERTY AND LOSS OF LIFE. It was an exaggeration. On the first day of the strike there were dozens of fistfights and numerous

cuts and bruises, and three shift bosses were hospitalized after being hit by flying rocks. But there was no property damage other than two broken windows, and no loss of life.

Nevertheless, Michigan governor Woodbridge Ferris believed the worst and reacted immediately with his most powerful weapon. He mobilized the entire 2,500-man state militia and ordered it to Copper Country. Headquartered at the Calumet armory—owned by C & H—the militia set up tents in front of the mines, on street corners, and on church lawns. The militia was not to take sides, but the presence of the troops allowed nonstriking workers to reopen some of the mines at 20 percent capacity.

At the same time, C & H created an organization called the Citizens' Alliance to show support for the mine owners and opposition to labor unions and strikes. Similar groups had been

Facing page:

(Top left) Striker's wife during the early days of the strike.

(Top right) Strikers marching east on Red Jacket Road. One striker holds a sign that reads FERRIS WILL HEAR FROM 1800 MINERS ON ELECTION DAY.

(Bottom) Strikers and their families marching north on Stanton Avenue in Calumet.

(Below) The state militia, ordered north by Michigan governor Woodbridge Ferris, arrives in Copper Country, July 1913.

State militia tents set up in front of C & H's company office (in background, behind pole). The building with the curved roof is the armory—later used as a prison for striking miners.

organized during previous strikes in the copper districts of Idaho and Montana, and the Colorado Citizens' Alliance was successful in curbing membership in the Western Federation of Miners in 1904. Calumet's Citizens' Alliance was to play an important role in the Michigan strike.

The formula for the Alliance was simple: With its extensive deposits of money, C & H controlled all the banks in Copper Country and, therefore, credit and the ability to do business. The butchers, bankers, merchants, and grocers who did not

support C & H and join the Citizens' Alliance could find their credit cut off and business failure staring them in the face. C & H also owned the land under their businesses.

As a voice for the Alliance, C & H created a newspaper called *Truth*. In it were printed membership applications to be filled out and mailed to the Alliance's headquarters in Houghton—or merchants could sign up in any bank. The Citizens' Alliance held mass meetings almost every day, and its slogan was, "The Western Federation of Miners Must Go!" Speakers worked crowds into a fever pitch in denouncing the WFM, and members were encouraged, whenever in public, to wear on their lapel a white button with the insignia CITIZENS' ALLIANCE.

In July some of the businessmen and shopkeepers in Calumet said that the miners were entitled to a fair deal. By August virtually all of them sported white buttons on their lapels and participated in rallies of the Citizens' Alliance. Some began cutting off credit to union members, saying no more purchases "on tick." As a local hotel clerk noted, "It's funny how quick the businessmen changed. Before the strike they said, 'If the miners strike, [the miners] are not to blame. They're entitled to a square deal.' But when James McNaughton said, 'The grass will grow on your streets before I'll ever give in,' they began to change. It's funny."

Alliance members set up roadblocks to try to stop Big Annie and the strikers from reaching the mines, but the strikers went around the roadblocks and reached the mines anyway. To Annie and all who participated, the demonstrations were solemn undertakings designed to touch the hearts of nonstriking workers—which they often did, causing some to drop their lunchpails and join the strike. One observer stated that when a working miner "would see the silent, determined men walking along the road in large numbers, men with whom he had worked, and he knew their conditions were the same as his . . . he would know that these men were trying to better his as well as their condition, [and] it would have a moral effect upon him."

Towering over most of the miners she led, Annie was described as "a tall, straight-backed woman, beaming confidence, and carrying a great silk flag bigger than herself." A reporter asked her if the big flag wasn't too heavy, and she answered, "I get used to it. I carried it ten miles one morning.

James T. O'Donnell, a superintendent of the Waddell-Mahon strikebreaking company, in Calumet.

The men wouldn't let me carry it any further. I love to carry it."

Even before Annie began leading the strikers around the roadblocks each day, Sheriff Cruse had moved secretly against them. Having already deputized a force of 150 men, Cruse hired employees of the Waddell-Mahon Company, a New York firm that specialized in supplying strikebreakers in labor disputes. Cruse had received secret approval for importing the strikebreakers from the County Board of Commissioners—whose chairman was James McNaughton. Recruited from the slums of New York, the fifty-two agents brought to Calumet were described as "strong-arm men, thugs, and murderers." The "Waddies," as they were called, were given complete authority and openly carried guns.

In the first week of the strike, miners felt the full weight of Cruse's deputies, the Waddies, and the militia. At Isle Royale a striker was shot in the leg by a soldier. At the Quincy mine a striker was shot in both legs after he refused to leave the property, and another was shot dead by Cruse's men. When sheriff's deputies tried to arrest a miner for assault on a nonstriking miner in Wolverine, 200 people rushed to the scene in the striking miner's defense but were beaten back by two squads of militiamen using bayonets. After the man was arrested, jailed, and beaten unconscious with brass knuckles, strikers hurled stones at the militia and exchanged blows with soldiers at Isle Royale and Red Jacket. More than 200 strikers were arrested and jailed in the first two weeks of the strike.

The militia commander, General Peter Abby, could not keep

Michigan governor
Woodbridge Ferris.

Militia officers, including General Peter Abby, who commanded the forces in Copper Country. (Abby's name is misspelled in a handwritten note on this news photograph.)

his men's presence neutral; when the soldiers were cursed or stoned, they retaliated. Nor could he control the personal behavior of his men. Residents complained about the drunkenness of the soldiers, and two intoxicated guardsmen beat up a man and tried to drag his 53-year-old wife into the bush before being stopped by a third soldier. The militia had been instructed to keep the streets clear of all gatherings; on July 31, soldiers on night patrol in Calumet drove people from their doorsteps with horses and used pick handles to force them inside. It was said that General Abby spent most of his time in the Calumet and Hecla clubhouse drinking champagne and smoking cigars while his troops ran rampant.

Compelled to act by complaints against the militia and by the miners' request for mediation, Governor Ferris journeyed to Copper Country early in August and conducted a three-day investigation of the dispute. He concluded that the militia and Cruse's deputies were responsible for the violence and stated publicly, "I do not hesitate to say that the [miners] have real grievances and grounds for complaint." Ferris suggested a conference between the mine owners and strikers; the owners said no. Ferris then appointed Judge Alfred Murphy to devise a plan of settlement, but after trying his best, Judge Murphy concluded that the owners would never recognize the miners' union or grant a pay raise, and that the one-man drill was here to stay. The judge called the mine owners "basically un-American." Ferris called them "arrogant and unfair" and, finding no evi-

Charles Moyer, president of the Western Federation of Miners.

dence of rioting or property destruction, ordered the gradual withdrawal of the militia.

The troops began to leave on August 11; by September 3 the force would be cut to 679 enlisted men and 64 officers. Increasingly the job of guarding the mines shifted to Sheriff Cruse's deputies, the Waddies, and Cruse's new recruits: strike-breakers from the Asher Agency in New York who boasted a record of having broken sixty-nine strikes before seeing action in Calumet. In July these men carried pick handles. By August they carried riot sticks the size of baseball bats, manufactured in the C & H carpentry shop.

Within days of the strike being called, Charles Moyer, the president of the Western Federation of Miners, had rushed to Copper Country to take control of the strike that he had advised against. But he had no more success in controlling the workers than Abby had in controlling the guard. Annie continued to lead the parade every morning, and afterward, around noon, the miners assembled at their headquarters in Dunn's Hall, where their leaders exhorted them in English, Finnish, Croatian, Italian, and Polish to stick together and "avoid all acts of violence." By August there was little chance of further violence being avoided. Under the direction of C & H and the company's manager, James McNaughton, Sheriff Cruse now commanded 3,000 armed men whose job it was to break the strike.

5 On the Scrap

On August 14, 1913 Sheriff Cruse sent two deputies and four Waddell men to a boardinghouse in Seeberville, south of Calumet. They went to arrest two strikers for walking across mine property on their way home. A struggle ensued and the strikers fled inside, whereupon the Waddell men and the deputies surrounded the boardinghouse and opened fire, shooting indiscriminately through doors and windows. When the gunfire stopped, two men had been killed and a baby in her mother's arms had been grazed in the face by a bullet. After warrants were issued for the arrest of the gunmen, they escaped to an adjoining county, where Cruse refused to go after them.

Along with other shootings and beatings carried out by the Waddies in August, the Seeberville murders captured the attention of the nation. Newspaper reporters from New York, Chicago, and other big cities poured into Copper Country to cover the strike, and major magazines such as *Collier's*, *Outlook*, and *Survey* sent writers for on-the-spot reports. In the first three weeks of the strike, more than a million words flowed out of the

(Top) The site of the Seeberville murders of August 14 in a photograph taken several months later. The killings drew nationwide attention to the plight of the strikers.

(Left) This man was injured during the shooting at the Seeberville boardinghouse.

telegraph offices at Houghton, Hancock, and Calumet, and film of the miners' parades was shown as far away as France, Germany, Italy, and Japan.

Famous people arrived to lend support for the strikers, adding more publicity to their cause. Clarence Darrow, one of the most renowned lawyers of the period, came to represent the miners in the lawsuits growing out of the strike. He marched with Big Annie. John Mitchell of the United Mine Workers of America addressed the strikers in Calumet and Houghton. He marched with Big Annie. Mother Jones, one of the most famous women of the times and the champion of American labor, marched with Big Annie on three occasions.

In August, Mother Jones conducted a six-day whirlwind tour. A thousand strikers applauded wildly as she stepped off the train at Red Jacket and refused a ride to the miners' head-

Labor leader Mother Jones during her visit to Calumet on August 10, 1913.

quarters. She said she would rather "march with the boys," which the eighty-three-year-old woman did under a banner that read RICHEST MINES, POOREST MINERS. In a fiery speech to an overflow crowd of 2,000, she denounced the mine owners for their stubbornness, praised the strikers for standing together, and told them not to drink or carry guns. She said, screaming from the pulpit, "Use your fist and black his two eyes, and then he can't see to shoot you!" Calumet had seen nothing like it.

Nor had the reporters, whose attention was captivated not by James McNaughton and C & H, not by Charles Moyer and the Western Federation of Miners, but by the heart and soul of the strike—Big Annie and the women of Calumet. Very early in the strike, on August 1, a striker told a reporter for the *Detroit Free Press* that if the strikers won, much of the credit would belong to the workers' wives, whom he called "the heart and

Lawyer Clarence Darrow fought numerous causes on behalf of labor unions during the first half of the twentieth century—including the Michigan copper miners.

John Mitchell, United Mine
Workers of America.

soul of the cause. They urged us to strike," he said, "and they're urging us not to give in."

From the beginning, the women were in the forefront of clashes with Cruse's men, the Waddies, and the militia. On July 31, when deputies arrested, jailed, and beat unconscious a miner at Wolverine, his wife showered the deputies with hot water and red pepper. In August, following the Seeberville killings, women marched on the mines at Quincy, Painesdale, and Calumet. They snatched lunchpails from nonstriking workers, spit at them, beat them with their fists, and pummeled them with eggs and tin cans. Later that month Fred Schneider, who had let his union membership expire, was attacked on his way to work by thirty women who tied his arms and splattered him with eggs while shouting, "We will fix you!" He told the soldiers who rescued him that a 250-pound woman held him down while others tried to scratch his eyes out.

At Painesdale in late August a striker's wife beat a nonstriking neighbor's wife with a broom dipped in human excrement. A week later, in early September, some seventy-five women marched on the outskirts of Calumet swinging brooms similarly dipped and causing General Abby to telegraph Governor Ferris requesting a declaration of martial law. Ferris said no and told Abby that the women had as much right to demonstrate as the men and that he had better move his troops out of the way. When Abby's soldiers seized Kate Rajkovich and Annie Papich—and their fouled brooms—twenty-five women followed them to the Calumet armory and tried to force their way in to free the prisoners. Only the sight of Abby's soldiers pointing rifles drove them back.

Women often rushed the automobiles of Cruse's deputies, and one reporter said it was common to see a nonstriking man with a bruised face show up for work, having been knocked down and beaten by women. Writing for *Survey* magazine, G. R. Taylor gave a delicate summary of the new activism: "In mass picketing and parades, women of the strikers' families are active. Not infrequently they attempt to snatch dinner pails away from scabs and sometimes, in addition to a tongue-lashing, they have applied to their victims a broom dipped in filth."

Inevitably, C & H was forced to turn Cruse's deputies, the Waddies, and what was left of the militia against the women, giving reporters sensational stories to tell. On September 2 in Calumet, Cruse's men fired on the women and a bullet hit fourteen-year-old Margaret Fazekas in the head. Margaret recovered—but typical of the reporters' stories was the one that read, "The deputies fired into a crowd of helpless women and children, killing a fourteen-year-old girl." On September 4, a woman flaying a broom and cursing was answered back by a guardsman, "I'll fix you so that you won't handle a broom anymore!" The guardsman tried to tie her to his horse and drag her on the ground while other women hammered him with rocks and sticks. Soldiers drove women off mine property at Red Jacket by "punching and hitting" them, reporters said, and in Laurium during one confrontation a militiaman rode his horse into the crowd and severely injured a small child. One reporter for a New York newspaper declared, "Houghton County is not a community of self-governing citizens. It is one chiefly of immigrants brought in to serve the monopoly, and ruled from Boston in defiance of the law and democratic institutions."

The strike might have ended after the Seeberville murders had it not been for the women of Copper Country. Against all the forces C & H controlled—Cruse's deputies, the Waddies, the state militia, the Citizens' Alliance—the women continued to march, believing that this was the only way they could better their lives. One woman marcher told a reporter as she pointed to her children, "These are the ones we are striking for. You don't want to see them bent and crippled before their time, do you?" Another woman, carrying a three-year-old child, told a newsman that two years earlier her husband had been killed in the mines, leaving her with four small children and a meager payment of fifteen dollars a month from Houghton County. "I must have more money, so I work at whatever I can," she said. "Strike not good. May be bad for men, but company no good either. Men killed, company pay nothing. Many families get poor by strike, but maybe men win. I hope so."

Indeed, the strike might have ended after a week had it not been for the image of Big Annie standing tall against Cruse's men; it was this image that caused women to dip their brooms and take to the streets of Calumet. The Citizens' Alliance called her a Communist, Sheriff Cruse called her a "radical agitator," and General Abby called her "that insane woman." But the reporters who followed her around emphasized her courage and grit and made her the focus of their stories, saying she was "on the scrap," meaning she was spoiling for a fight if anyone dared stop her. Writing for *Outlook* magazine, Inis Weed reported, "Again and again the guards have tried to incite the strikers to violence by breaking into their sunrise parades. But no lengths of brutality daunt the spirit of these workers, led by Big Annie, a tall, handsome Croatian woman, who holds a flag across her breast and defies her assailants to kill her when they beat her."

Annie headed the funeral processions for the victims of the Seeberville murders and led other women in confrontations with the forces of C & H. On September 10, she was arrested with five other women who tried to stop a man from going to work and got into fistfights with Cruse's deputies sent to the rescue. A crowd of 300 followed Annie and the women to the Calumet jail and cheered wildly after their release two hours later.

On September 13, Annie led 1,000 strikers and women through Calumet to the corner of Eighth and Elm, where they were confronted by guardsmen and deputies armed with

Big Annie led the funeral procession through Calumet for the Seeberville murder victims. Ten girls dressed in white followed a white hearse carrying the body of eighteen-year-old Alais Tijan. The second hearse carried the body of Steve Patrick.

swords, guns, and clubs. When Annie walked head-on into the troops, a soldier on horseback unsheathed his saber and knocked the flag from her hands. A marcher went to help her pick up the staff, but a cavalryman pushed him to the ground and another soldier slashed at the flag with his sword, ripping the silk fabric. Annie was knocked to the ground as horses stomped the flag into the mud. Lying in the mud, she hugged the flag to her chest as soldiers tried to rip it away from her.

"Kill me!" she shouted. "Run your bayonets and sabers

through this flag and kill me, but I won't move. If this flag will not protect me, then I will die with it." Other marchers rescued her, and she escaped unharmed. But over and over, as the bitter strike stretched into autumn, Annie confronted the cavalry and Cruse's men. She spit at them, kicked them, and swung at them with her soiled broom. She was arrested three times and spent ten days in jail. During one of her arrests General Abby asked her why she didn't just stay at home. "I won't stay at home," she replied. "My work is here, and nobody can stop me. I'm going to keep at it until this strike is won." She kicked the police car and pounded it with her fists as Abby pushed her in for the ride to jail. Later she told reporters that this was her first ride in an automobile, and she was proud of the occasion.

Almost without exception, the reporters who covered Annie and the parades said they were peaceful and blamed the guard and deputies for provoking violence. Because it was widely rumored that the Waddies had been told to provoke violence if they wished to keep their jobs, Houghton County hired a detective who posed as a striker to gain firsthand knowledge of the Waddies. He reported that the Waddies cursed and provoked the marchers and termed their behavior "very brutal." One reporter predicted that Annie would be murdered by the Waddies to stop the strike. A member of the Citizens' Alliance echoed the sentiments of C & H: "Damn it, these parades every morning on the village streets have got to stop!" But the parades continued.

They continued because the strikers vowed to follow Big Annie until the strike was won. They called her "an American Joan of Arc." They said, "This woman is the kind all red-blooded men could take their hats off to." At the age of eighty Annie's brother Frank recalled that "Annie was something else. She believed in her cause. She wouldn't back off, no matter how much pressure they put on her. She said the men were fighting for dignity and self-respect." Ted Taipalus, a thirteen-year-old at the time, recalled: "I'll always remember Big Annie carrying the flag and leading the parade." While women were swinging brooms and their husbands were being beaten in jail, and while Annie herself was in jail, the *Miner's Bulletin* ran the following story filed by N. D. Cochran. As much as any other account, it captured the spirit, the verve, the heart, and the grit of the woman from Calumet:

> I have met Annie Clemenc. I have talked with her. I have seen her marching along the middle of the street, carrying that great American flag. She is a striking figure, strong, with firm but supple muscles, fearless, ready to die for a cause.
>
> A militia officer said to me, "If McNaughton could only buy Big Annie, he could break the strike." I don't believe all the millions of dividends taken out of the Calumet and Hecla mine could buy her.
>
> I walked fully two miles with her . . . and I thought what glorious men and women America would produce if there were millions of mothers like Annie Clemenc. I thought that one Annie Clemenc, miner's wife, was worth thousands of James McNaughtons.
>
> Annie Clemenc is more of an American in my esteem than the spineless but well-meaning governor of Michigan. And as manhood goes, she's more of a man in

fighting quality, in sand, in courage, in heroism than Governor Ferris.

If Annie Clemenc is in that dirty little jail now, the American flag would be better off on top of that jail than over some courthouse. Where she is there is love of liberty and courage to fight for it. Annie Clemenc isn't afraid to die.

6 Papa Is Striking for Us

Guns, swords, clubs, and charging horses had failed to stop Big Annie and the mass parades. By mid-September Cruse's deputies had killed four strikers, two at Seeberville and two others in separate confrontations, and hope for an early settlement of the strike had vanished. Big Annie and other women of the Western Federation of Miners Auxiliary No. 15 erected white crosses on poles and street signs where the strikers had been killed.

After a six-week investigation, Walter Palmer of the U.S. Department of Labor concluded, "Most of the violence has been provoked by armed deputies imported by the mining companies" and "Many of the mines are entirely lacking in proper safety and sanitation." He proposed that a settlement be reached by a committee of five people, two to be chosen by the mine owners, two by the strikers, and one by the government. The strikers accepted the plan; the owners said no. Nonunion men who were also striking made a move to go back to work by electing a committee that went to see James McNaughton. They would go back to work for three dollars a day with two men

Flier warning outside workers to stay away from Copper Country.

working the one-man drill. McNaughton said no; the men had to return to work unconditionally, and only then would he listen to any pleas they might have. C & H would not budge an inch.

The strike had become an endurance test between C & H and the workers. Earlier, James McNaughton had said, "No outside workers will be imported by the Calumet and Hecla," but by mid-September the company was importing outside workers, many of them recent immigrants to America living in the tenements of New York. To counter this move, the strikers sent out a network of men to tell the foreigners about the strike and warn them about the widow-maker. They had some success. Hungarians talked to Hungarians, Finns to Finns, and some of the immigrants jumped off the trains en route to Calumet. Others left the mines after working only a few days saying, as one did, "I not know strike. I not work against union." Strikers tried to stop the trains carrying the new workers, but ultimately some 1,500 men were imported and put to work, the cost of their transportation and clothing being deducted from their wages.

Members of the Citizens' Alliance who were merchants and grocers stepped up the pressure by suspending all credit to strikers, while other Alliance members closed their businesses completely. In a protest against the merchants, Annie led a demonstration past their stores, each member wearing a Citizens' Alliance button pinned to the backside of pants or dresses. By mid-September some nonunion men had returned to work, joining the replacement workers who continued to arrive, but the Calumet and Hecla mines still ran at less than 25 percent capacity. And the parades continued every day behind a large American flag.

Consequently, C & H tried to stop the parades with the one institution in Copper Country it did not control: the courts. Accusing the strikers of trespassing and interfering with a person's right to work, the company's team of seven lawyers asked Judge Patrick O'Brien on September 20 for a sweeping injunction to make any demonstration, which in any way might interfere with C & H's operation, illegal. O'Brien granted a temporary order but revoked it on September 29 after C & H failed to produce evidence of the strikers' violating anyone's rights. He

P.H. O'Brien,
Circuit Judge

Judge Patrick O'Brien, whose father died in the C & H mines, and who consistently made rulings supporting the strikers' right to demonstrate against C & H.

said the strikers had the right to parade and persuade men not to work if they did so peacefully.

After O'Brien rejected a second appeal for an injunction, the C & H lawyers carried the fight to Michigan's Supreme Court, which ordered O'Brien to reinstate the September 20 injunction. He did, but when the first group of strikers arrested for violating the order appeared in his court, he released the 141 men and women and advised Sheriff Cruse not to arrest any more strikers for violating the injunction. Cruse ignored the advice and arrested another group of 139 strikers. O'Brien pronounced the strikers guilty—then suspended their sentences, thereby infuriating C & H's lawyers, company manager McNaughton, and Sheriff Cruse. O'Brien declared that they had broken the law "through enthusiasm for their cause rather than with any intention of deliberately violating the order of the court."

The strikers were "engaged in a heroic struggle for the mere right to retain membership in a labor organization," O'Brien said. "To agitate for improved conditions is the right of any citizen." He added that C & H had done nothing to satisfy the workers but everything to "increase their bitterness and hostility." Judge O'Brien had been born and raised in Copper Country. He had firsthand knowledge of who was responsible for the violence. And his father had been killed in the Calumet and Hecla mines. C & H's lawyers were wasting their time in Judge Patrick O'Brien's court.

Meanwhile, the violence continued. On October 1, Annie was leading 400 strikers to the mines when they were intercepted by deputies and cavalrymen commanded by Major Harry Britton, who called the women "ringleaders in terrorizing families." When Britton tried to arrest Annie for spitting at a workman, another striker wrestled with the major and forced him to release Annie. Britton drew his sword and struck the man, and soon clubs, stones, and fists were flying in every direction as the cavalrymen charged into the ranks of the strikers. "Excited horses prancing about are the best weapons," the major said, after he described "a striker with his head bleeding, blood flowing down over his shirt, half-staggering along the road." Annie and nine others were arrested, but the next day she was leading a demonstration.

On October 6, 8, and 9, Annie led parades accompanied by 500 children who skipped school in the face of truancy notices to show support for their parents. One boy carried a hand-lettered sign that read Papa Is Striking for Us, and reporters were quick to seize upon the story. 500 Young Sympathizers with Striking Miners Refuse to Study read the headline in

Children parading in support of their striking parents.

A marching child carries a sign proclaiming PAPA IS STRIKING FOR US. The phrase made headlines nationwide.

the *New York Times,* and the reporter wrote, "The sympathetic strike of schoolchildren in the Keweenaw County copper strike spread this morning, and 500 refused to study."

Parading in a blizzard of snow on November 8, Annie and ninety-nine others were arrested and incarcerated in C & H's armory, since Calumet's jail was now at capacity. Nine days later deputies fired seventy shots into a parade of demonstrators, wounding three and splattering blood on the snow. From October 23 to November 15, more than 400 strikers were arrested and jailed. Most of them, including Big Annie, were released after serving only a few days, or in some cases only a few hours, by order of Judge O'Brien. On the other side, only four people were ever sent to jail for crimes against the strikers—two Waddies and two of Cruse's deputies; all four were eventually arrested and convicted for the Seeberville murders.

As the strike stretched into December, the Citizens' Alliance became the main instrument used to stop Big Annie and the parades. Clarence Darrow, the union's lawyer, petitioned Judge O'Brien for an injunction against the Citizens' Alliance for violence against the strikers. O'Brien found the Alliance members guilty of harassing and attacking strikers and granted the order prohibiting Alliance members from interfering with the parades. But the ruling wasn't issued until December 24, well after the Citizens' Alliance went into a frenzy over the Painesdale murders of December 7.

In the early morning hours of December 7, several men with high-powered rifles fired some forty rounds into a boardinghouse in Painesdale where strikebreakers lived. Three were killed in their beds, and the gunmen were never caught or identified. The strikers were the obvious culprits, but the union's president, Charles Moyer, denied any involvement, saying this was an old trick used to discredit strikers. Perhaps he was right. Following the strike during a congressional investigation, Richard Maher, one of the Waddies, swore by affidavit that the Waddies were hired to break up the parades by any means. "We had suggestions made to us that the job was getting too quiet," he said, "and that we should go out and start something. Our standing order was to shoot the first man that came near our sight on the highway which ran near the company's property. We were informed that we could go as far as we liked and that the sheriff would not interfere with us." The investigator assigned to the Painesdale case also believed that the murders were committed by Waddies in an effort to turn public opinion against the strikers.

Nevertheless, C & H and the Citizens' Alliance blamed the murders on Judge O'Brien because of his leniency and on unidentified strikers. Holding a mass assembly in Calumet on the afternoon of December 7, the Citizens' Alliance passed a resolution proclaiming its demand "to rid this community of these murder-inciting mercenaries."

Members armed themselves and accompanied Cruse's deputies in a series of raids. On December 11, they raided the strikers' headquarters in South Range and fought a gun battle, but the strikers held their ground. Although the details were sketchy, the Grand Rapids *Herald* reported, "A pitched rifle battle between deputy sheriffs and the Citizens' Alliance on one side and striking copper-miners on the other raged all day on South Range." Alliance members also helped deputies search the homes of striking miners, confiscating twenty rifles, four revolvers, and six swords from twelve houses. The owners protested that they used the rifles for hunting, while Italians protested the confiscation of their ceremonial lodge swords. Once again Alliance members erected barricades across streets to block the strikers from the mines.

Annie continued to lead the parades every morning, now

often accompanied by Clarence Darrow and by Frank Shavs, a reporter for a Chicago newspaper. Shortly after his arrival in Calumet, Shavs had abandoned his objectivity in reporting the strike and had joined it. Attracted by the tall, independent woman leading the strikers and their wives, Frank often marched with Annie, and their relationship grew closer.

But by mid-December, with the arrival of freezing cold and snow, prospects for winning the strike appeared dim. The strike benefits promised by Moyer and the national union had failed to materialize. The strikers had to rely on donations of food and clothing from the Associated Charities and the Salvation Army. To feed and care for their families, some men were forced to go back to work in the mines. Others left Copper Country for employment elsewhere, believing that the strike was now destined to fail. For the same reason, reporters began to leave. C & H's hospital was now closed to the strikers, their wives, and their children. McNaughton had issued an ultimatum: If the men did not return to work by December 19, they would be permanently replaced by other workers.

At the same time, C & H threatened to evict some striking miners from their homes. Some were told to return to work or start paying twenty-five dollars a month for rent, instead of the normal six dollars. When Croatian miner Louis Zargnal received such a notice, he said he would pay his full rent when he returned to work—after the strike was won. Nor did a threat to turn off his electricity bother him: "I say that is nothing," Louis intoned. "Lots of kerosene. Burn lamp with kerosene." On December 5 his electricity and water were cut off, and Louis, his family, and their furniture were "tossed out in the snow."

But in December, 7,000 men, including Louis Zargnal, were still out on strike. After five months, Big Annie had marched nearly 1,000 miles and she was still leading the parade every morning carrying the American flag. For a time it seemed as if nothing could stop her.

7 Silent Night

As Christmas approached, Annie and the miners sloshed through the snow in darkness each morning and sang Christmas carols standing in a circle around the C & H mines. James McNaughton's December 19 deadline fell on deaf ears. Strikers evicted from their homes moved in with other families, and the men often blocked Cruse's deputies and the Citizens' Alliance from conducting household raids.

By December, Annie had been elected president of the Western Federation of Miners Auxiliary No. 15. To lift everyone's spirits, especially the children's, she organized a Christmas party to be held on December 24. Heading a committee of four women, she raised funds to buy gifts so that each child would have a present to open. Miners in New Jersey sent twenty-five dollars for the party, Calumet residents contributed another sixty-four dollars, and the local union gave its last funds, $57.25. The women spent weeks sewing scarves and mittens, making little bags of candy, and rehearsing a Mother Goose play, and one of the strikers volunteered to play Santa Claus. Because there was so little money, the three Christmas trees secured for the occasion could be decorated only with discarded crepe paper and ten cents' worth of tinsel.

Annie made arrangements to hold the party on the second floor of Italian Hall, where the strikers often met and where they also held dances and other social activities. It was one of Calumet's newer buildings, having been constructed in 1908 after the old Italian Hall caught fire and burned to the ground. A grocery store and a saloon occupied the first floor. An eight-foot-wide stairway consisting of twenty-two steps led to the ballroom on the second floor, which was complete with a stage and a small kitchen. The Citizens' Alliance charged that the dances held by the Auxiliary in the ballroom were designed to spread Socialist propaganda.

From all parts of the mining community, children and their parents tramped through the snow, some two or three miles, to reach Italian Hall. By two o'clock more than 500 children and about 175 adults had arrived, and the ballroom was alive with the activities of Christmas. Women were in the kitchen cutting saffron cake. Men were cracking open barrels of chocolate-drop candies. Theresa Sizer played Christmas songs on the piano, and the children sang carols in four different languages. But they were so anxious to get their presents that the Mother Goose play was postponed. Yelling and stretching out their arms, the children were pressed twenty deep against the stage, where Big Annie directed Santa in distributing the gifts.

Then someone shouted, "Fire! Fire!"

Instantly, panic swept the hall—the crowd surged toward the stairwell. Theresa Sizer was standing near the man who had yelled "Fire!" Realizing the danger of his words, she shook the man by his shoulders and said, "What are you saying! There is

Italian Hall, scene of the miners' Christmas party.

no fire! Sit down! Sit down!" He escaped her grasp and ran away. Seeing no smoke or sign of fire, Annie quickly sized up the situation and from the stage began screaming that there was no fire. At the same time, a man who tried to shout from the street below that there was no fire was clubbed on the head.

Miner John Auno was standing on the landing at the top of the stairs when he heard a man's voice shout "Fire!" from inside the hall. He turned to look inside but was immediately hit by a wall of bodies that pushed him down the stairs and knocked him unconscious. "They all started to come out," John said. "Some went rolling down, and some were running down over them." Another striker was also at the top of the stairway and tried to stop the stampede: "But it was impossible," he said. "The way the women and children were screaming, it was almost impossible to make your voice heard. It was just a moving mass down the stairs."

Some of the people who reached the bottom of the stairs first stumbled and fell; others stumbled and fell on top of the first group, and within minutes the stairway was blocked. At the bottom people were "jammed into one solid mass from which no one could emerge," but others continued to hurtle down, clawing over the tangle of bodies. "The only way you could breathe in the hallway," said Walter Lahti, who was thirteen years old at the time, "was to push yourself off the wall with all your might and then quickly suck in a breath of air before the force of the other bodies pushed your face back against the wall." Suffocating to death as he stood upright on the stairs, Abe Niemala, age twenty-four, saved his six-month-old baby by hoisting the child high in the air with both arms and standing in a locked position. Another father gave up his life in exactly the same way and saved his infant son, but John Saari, age five, was not so lucky. His father was carrying him and another child when they were knocked down and crushed to death.

When the first firemen and rescue workers arrived, even the strongest of the men were forced to turn their eyes. At the bottom of the stairway they found bodies piled four and five feet high, twisted together so tightly that it was impossible to untangle them. Instead, the rescue workers used ladders and climbed through the windows on the second floor, and then began removing bodies in the stairwell from the top downward. The pile of bodies extended almost thirty feet toward the top of the stairs. Children were screaming to be rescued from beneath the pile and crying from terrible pain. It took an hour to clear the stairway.

Doctors said that in most cases death was instantaneous. The children died from ruptured arteries or crushed organs; their heads were crushed, their chests caved in. The adults died from suffocation. In less than three minutes, seventy-four people died in the stairwell; all but eleven were children. Reporters who witnessed the scene found that words were inadequate to describe the horror in Italian Hall.

Within an hour a crowd of 5,000 had assembled, and the militia, Cruse's deputies, and members of the Citizens' Alliance formed a cordon to hold them back. At first, parents who had not attended the party, but whose children had, broke through the line screaming and crying. But deputies on horseback charged the crowd and held it at bay while other deputies on foot beat back the crowd with riot sticks. Eventually a lane was opened through the crowd, and more than fifty automobiles transported the bodies to a temporary morgue at Red Jacket's town hall. The children were placed on long tables and on the floor of the banquet room, where they remained until each was identified. The line of parents, relatives, neighbors, and schoolmates stretched for more than a mile into the winter darkness of Calumet.

As the victims were removed, Annie sat on the stage holding a dead child she had desperately tried to revive with water. She told reporters that a man wearing a Citizens' Alliance button had entered the hall and cried, "Fire!" Other survivors said the same thing, and as reporters told the world of the tragedy, they attributed it to the Citizens' Alliance. One resident of Milwaukee wrote in her diary on December 27: "A terrible thing has occurred among the miners at Calumet. Eighty of their children were killed in a panic started by the Citizens' Alliance." Some believed that Annie was the target and that the Alliance aimed to kill everyone in the hall to stop the strike. A Finnish lady said, after she saw the mounted deputies below, the police "were going to put them in traps and kill everybody."

Sympathy telegrams from around the world poured into Calumet as the strikers prepared to bury their dead. Their grief was only matched by their anger toward C & H and the Citizens' Alliance. At news of the tragedy, company manager McNaughton went to Italian Hall, offered the services of the company's hospital, and told reporters, "This is the most awful calamity that has ever been known in Calumet, and the sympathy of all goes out to members of the bereaved families." Union president Moyer would have none of it, and, calling the disaster "mass murder," he blamed it squarely on the mine owners and the Citizens' Alliance. More than twenty eyewitnesses told him it was an Alliance man who had yelled "Fire!"

The Alliance denied any involvement, and to offset its tarnished image, the organization raised $25,000 to aid families of the victims. But when the funds were delivered to Moyer, he refused the offering outright, calling it blood money: "We will bury our own dead," he said. He and the strikers believed that members of the Citizens' Alliance had cheered as deputies blocked efforts to rescue the dying—although this was a baseless rumor.

The snow that had fallen since Christmas blanketed Calumet on December 28, when the funerals were held. Services were conducted in five different churches in the native tongue of each nationality. They lasted six hours, and afterward a procession was held from the churches to the cemetery, where most of the victims were buried in a mass grave dug by the strikers—in one of the few plots of land not owned by C & H. Hearses and funeral wagons carried the adults. Fathers and brothers carried

Funeral procession for the seventy-four victims of the Italian Hall disaster.

the white coffins of the children, and more than 50,000 mourners took part in the five-mile-long procession to the cemetery. Carrying the heavy flag she had carried so many times before, Annie Clemenc led the procession with tears streaming from her eyes.

One of the hearses that carried victims of the Italian Hall disaster to the gravesite, December 28, 1913.

Gravesite of the Italian Hall
disaster victims.

8 The Stillness at Calumet

The inquest into the Italian Hall tragedy was scheduled to begin on December 30. It was preceded by more bloodshed, bloodshed that did not diminish the grief of Calumet.

On the night of December 25, Sheriff Cruse went to see Moyer in his hotel room in Hancock. Cruse warned Moyer that if he did not take back his charge that an Alliance man had caused the panic, the sheriff would not be responsible for his future safety. Moyer ordered him out. Minutes later, approximately twenty-five men, most of them openly wearing Alliance buttons and the others Waddell agents, stormed into Moyer's room. They beat him, shot him in the back with a handgun, then dragged him more than a mile through the streets to the railway station. Along the route they took turns kicking him, and Alliance members standing on the roadside shouted "Hang him!" and "Lynch him!" Some were waving a hangman's noose.

Moyer was thrown onto a Chicago-bound train and told never to return to Copper Country. Bleeding badly and barely able to move, he survived the bullet wound and from his hospital bed in Chicago told the nation's press what had happened. Although the charge was never proved, he was insistent in claiming that McNaughton was at the train station and told him that if he ever came back he would be hanged. No one was ever charged in Moyer's assault and kidnapping, and there was no local investigation.

After Moyer was beaten and shot, a rumor spread that the real reason the Alliance had tried to kill him was because he had learned what had happened at Italian Hall. It was rumored that Moyer had found out that deputies held the doors shut and clubbed people as they tried to leave. The inquest would show that this was not the case, but hatred and mistrust ran so deep that strikers accepted the rumor as truth. When Alliance members went door-to-door offering the $25,000 they had raised, they could not give away a single cent. Most families refused the aid quietly. Others greeted the visitors with insults and ordered them out, shouting to families nearby, "Don't take any-

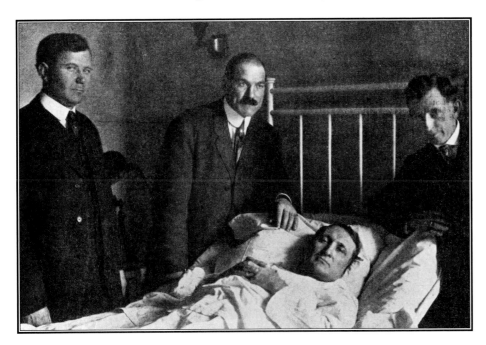

Charles Moyer recuperating at St. Luke's Hospital, Chicago, after being beaten, shot, and thrown onto a Chicago-bound train. Alongside him are (*from left to right*) John Walker, Illinois Federation of Labor; Yanco Terzich, Western Federation of Miners Executive Board member; and M. J. Riley, Western Federation of Miners representative.

thing from the blackhand." Another insisted: "It is not charity we want, it is justice." In one home where a man lay dead, Annie was comforting his widow when the visitors knocked at the door. She cursed and spit at them, then grabbed her broom and chased them into the street.

It was in this atmosphere of grief, hatred, and a numbness of feeling that the inquest was held. The accounts were straight-forward and sullen. Of the seventy witnesses who testified, eighteen said they had heard someone shout "Fire!" Nine of the witnesses said they had seen the man who shouted the alarm, and six of the nine said he had worn a white button.

Mary Coscalla was among them. "The way it started," she told coroner William Fisher, "a man came to the door and he hollered 'Fire!' and everyone started to rush." She said he was dressed all in black. He wore a black hat and a black overcoat with its high collar turned up, and he wore a white button, but she was too far away to tell what was written on it. Thirteen-year-old John Burcar was walking from the stage to a side window for a breath of fresh air when he almost bumped into the man in the overcoat. When the coroner asked, "What attracted your attention to him?" John replied, "The Citizens' Alliance pin he had on." When asked, "What did he say?" John answered, "He hollered, 'Fire!'" The testimony continued for three days, but the sorrow that had enveloped Calumet made the inquest seem almost moot.

Annie testified that she had not actually seen the man who yelled "Fire!"; she said that her account was based on reports from several eyewitnesses. Her responses were short and impassive. "She never was the same after the tragedy of Italian Hall," Annie's brother Frank said. "She never forgave. She

The stairway of Italian Hall, where the disaster occurred.

didn't like to talk about the Italian Hall disaster. It was a real sore spot with her. But she always thought it was the Citizens' Alliance that was responsible." Annie told Frank, "I was there. I know what happened."

The man who yelled "Fire!" was never identified. Avoiding any mention of the Citizens' Alliance, the inquest jury concluded, "The stampede was caused by some person unknown to the jury at this time, raising the alarm of fire within the hall." But

Interior of Italian Hall the morning after the tragedy.

indirectly the jury cleared the Citizens' Alliance of any blame. It noted that only people producing a union card or being vouched for by a union member were allowed into the party. Yet according to direct testimony given at the inquest, this was not true. At the start of the party union cards were carefully checked, but the crowd became so large and there was so much confusion that latecomers entered the ballroom without showing any identification. Even patrons of the saloon below testified that they walked up the stairs and entered the hall unchallenged.

Who was the man in the dark overcoat with his collar turned up? None of the eyewitnesses identified him as a striker or an acquaintance. Was the white button he wore a Citizens' Alliance button? Eric Erickson testified that he saw two men wearing Alliance buttons in the doorway just after the call of "Fire!" and John Burcar testified that he saw the white button the man was wearing and that it read CITIZENS' ALLIANCE. Mrs. Bert Czabo and Mrs. Anna Lustig said the same thing. Why was the man who tried to shout a warning from the street below clubbed on the head? Why was Moyer's kidnapping not investigated, when dozens of witnesses could identify by name the Alliance members and the Waddies who beat and shot the president of the Western Federation of Miners? Most important of all, why would anyone shout "Fire!" when there was no fire? These were questions residents would ask, and future generations in Calumet would ask, for the next eighty years—and answer in their own minds: The Citizens' Alliance was responsible.

The Italian Hall tragedy did what all else had failed to do. Tough men with faces hardened from months of bitter strike activity wept openly. Mothers and children who had dutifully marched each morning hugged one another tightly to fight the pain. Others withdrew inward. Still more could not talk about it, as if to do so would lessen the enormity of the tragedy. Silently, with tears that would not cease, the families turned away from Italian Hall. The parades stopped.

Many workers believed that even if they won the strike now, a return to the mines would be an act of personal treason. They piled on trains by the hundreds and looked out the windows with blank stares at the replacement workers on trains filing into Calumet. Vowing never again to enter a mine, many headed for Detroit, where Henry Ford had just introduced a five-dollar-a-day wage for automobile workers. By March 1914, as many as 850 people a week were leaving Calumet.

Annie and 4,000 or so miners stayed behind and saw the strike to its conclusion. Following the Italian Hall tragedy, a congressional committee was sent to Copper Country, and it conducted hearings throughout most of February and March of 1914. It took testimony from striking miners, nonstriking workers, and officials of C & H. In its concluding report, the committee blamed the Waddies and C & H for most of the violence in the strike and declared conditions in the mines unhealthy and unsafe.

Forced to act because of pressure from the government committee, C & H offered its workers an eight-hour day and a three-dollar-a-day wage but refused to recognize the Western Federation of Miners or return to the two-man drill. On Sunday, April 13, the strike officially ended when the miners voted 3,104 to 1,636 to return to work under the new conditions. Although they had failed on the important issues of union recognition, a shorter workweek, and the widow-maker, most accepted the modest improvement in working conditions as a partial victory. On Monday, April 14, they returned to work and turned in their union cards at the mine entrances as a condition of employment. The Calumet and Hecla Mining Company resumed full operations, and Calumet returned to normal—that is, C & H resumed control.

In January, Annie served a ten-day jail sentence for a previous conviction of assault on a nonstriking miner. She was visited by Frank Shavs—but not by her husband, who vacated their house before Annie returned from jail. In February and March she traveled through the Midwest on a speaking tour to raise funds for the survivors of Italian Hall and also to interest other workers in joining a union for the common cause of labor. When she left for the lecture tour on February 26, local women showed up at the Calumet depot and presented Annie with a stylish feathered hat. Amid cheers, tears, and good wishes, she shouted at them as the train pulled away, "Of course we would rather die than give up!" After her tour and the vote to end the strike, she followed Frank Shavs to Chicago to begin a new life and to try to put the past behind her.

James McNaughton had said he would teach the miners to eat potato parings. Annie made him eat those words. She taught C & H that people could only be pushed so far. She taught C & H that women, as well as men, could be brave in fighting injustice. And by her example she demonstrated that there was nobility and magnificence in marching for a cause. She never regretted her role in the strike. She stayed to the end, as she had said she would, and helped win an improvement in working conditions. Though it struck her like a bullet through the heart, the tragedy at Italian Hall was not her fault, but the fault of parties unknown. Hers was the legacy of a tall woman marching and carrying an American flag for the cause of human rights. Hers was the legacy of America.

9 America

The Michigan copper miners, and the thousands of other workers who went on strike during the Industrial Revolution, established a tradition in America of demanding an honest day's wage for an honest day's work. In doing so, they asserted their rights as American citizens: the right to free speech, the right to protest, the right to assembly, the right to organize for a cause, and the right to petition government to correct a wrong.

The assertion of these same rights helped cause the American Revolution in 1776, helped bring about the abolition of slavery in 1865, helped win for women the right to vote in 1920, and helped end racial segregation and discrimination in the law in the 1960s. The industrial workers shared a common heritage with Roger Williams, who protested against forced worship and the mistreatment of Native Americans in 1636; with Henry Thoreau, who was jailed in 1846 when he refused to pay his taxes because they were used to support slavery; and with Mary Lease, the radical agitator from Kansas who fought the railroad monopolies in the 1890s on behalf of small farmers, saying the farmers should "Raise less corn and more Hell."

That heritage—of American citizens exercising their rights for a cause—has lasted for more than 200 years and has helped promote the growth of freedom and democracy.

In their time the abolitionists were beaten, smeared with tar, and run out of town; but slavery ended. Roger Williams was kicked out of Massachusetts for championing religious freedom and the cause of Native Americans; but he founded Rhode Island, where there was freedom of worship and where the Native Americans' right to land was recognized. During the Industrial Revolution, hundreds of workers died and thousands more were shot or maimed in the fierce clashes between strikers and corporate forces; but the workers ultimately won.

Midway through the Industrial Revolution, 10,000 workers marched through Union Square in New York City in the first Labor Day parade, on September 5, 1882. They carried placards that read THE TRUE REMEDY IS UNIONIZATION and 8 HOURS OF WORK, 8 HOURS OF REST—8 HOURS OF WHAT WE WILL! By 1894, 32 states had made September 5 a Labor Day holiday, and President Grover Cleveland declared it a national holiday. Organized at about the same time as the first Labor Day parade, the American Federation of Labor made plans to pressure business and government for the recognition of unions, higher wages, a shorter workday, and better working conditions. Its first president, Samuel Gompers, simplified these demands. When asked what the organization wanted, he replied, "More and more, here and now."

Membership in the American Federation of Labor grew steadily through the decades; it had many affiliates, including the Western Federation of Miners and Michigan's Auxiliary No. 15, whose president was Big Annie of Calumet. Along with

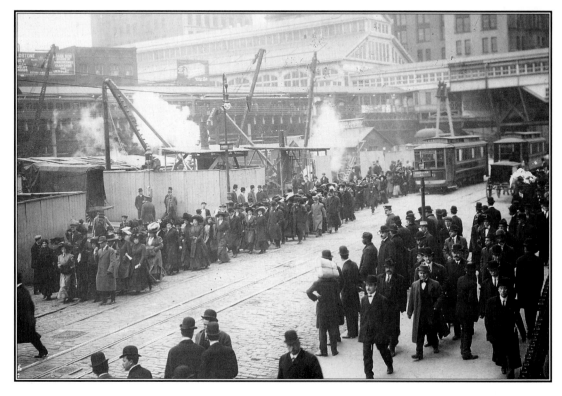

other national unions, such as the Knights of Labor and the United Mine Workers of America, the American Federation of Labor was influential in improving conditions for workers in numerous industries. With the backing of the Federation, carpenters started a campaign in 1890 for an eight-hour day; within a year they had won an eight-hour day in 137 cities.

Others in the building trades joined in, and by the early 1890s many skilled workers were working fewer hours and earning more. A report by the U.S. Industrial Commission in 1902 also aided the drive for an eight-hour day. Its investigation showed that excessive hours of labor resulted in less production, inferior quality of work, greater costs of operation, and

Pages 86-89:

Organized labor in New York City at the turn of the century:

(Facing page, top) Women delegates to 1886 Knights of Labor convention.

(Facing page, bottom) Garment workers' strike, about 1900.

(Below) Women's Trade Union League Chapter at the 1905 Labor Day parade.

(Right and below) Labor Day
parades, about 1910.

sickness and absenteeism for workers. Businessmen took note of the report's main conclusion: an eight-hour day was beneficial to both labor and management.

Another study, done in the 1920s by the National Industrial Conference Board, promoted the change from a six-day to a five-day workweek. Having studied ninety-four companies with a five-day workweek, the board declared, "It appears that nearly 70 percent of these companies have suffered no loss in total output per week and are obtaining greater production . . . This seems to indicate that [under a five-day workweek] management is actually achieving a greater profit."

Signs in Italian, Yiddish, and English at a protest for an eight-hour workday, 1918.

What the automaker Henry Ford had known for some time was becoming clearer and clearer to many employers: that the owners and the workers were in the same business and had a common interest. In a down-to-earth reporting of this truth, Henry Ford wrote an article in 1926 entitled "Why I Favor Five Days' Work with Six Days' Pay." "Now we know," he said gingerly, "in changing from six to five days and back again that we get at least as great production in five days as we can in six, and we shall probably get a greater, for the pressure will bring better methods. A full week's wage for a short week's work will pay." Ford's advice was not heeded by all employers, and many were forced into a five-day workweek by the thousands of strikes that continued well into the 1920s and 1930s. Some conceded the eight-hour day but wouldn't budge on the six-day workweek—as was the case with the Calumet and Hecla Mining Company.

Another goal for labor unions was the passage of laws providing compensation for injuries suffered on the job. The drive for workmen's compensation found a powerful ally in Theodore Roosevelt, who was president of the United States from 1901 to 1909. He denounced employers for their opposition to workmen's compensation legislation, saying that such opposition was "unjust and inhumane." Roosevelt thundered, "It is revolting that the financial burden of accidents occurring from work . . . should be thrust upon those sufferers who are least able to bear it." Following the president's leadership on the issue, in 1902 Maryland became the first state to enact a compensation law for injuries of workers in mining and railroad transportation.

What followed was a prolonged campaign to influence other

state lawmakers to pass similar compensation laws. Exercising their democratic right to effect change through their representatives, workers pledged to support the reelection of officeholders if they supported compensation laws. Success came in 1909 when Montana passed a compensation law for most workers in the state, and by 1922 Arkansas, Florida, North Carolina, and South Carolina were the only states without such laws. At Roosevelt's urging, in 1908 Congress passed the Federal Employers' Liability Act, providing compensation for government workers injured or killed on the job.

The long, bloody struggle between industrial workers and their employers culminated in the 1930s and 1940s during the Great Depression and President Franklin D. Roosevelt's New Deal. Early in his administration the president called for "a change from starvation wages and starvation employment to living wages and sustained employment," and he set about to achieve the goal. Under Roosevelt's direction and with the support of labor, Congress passed the National Industrial Recovery Act (NIRA) in 1933. Along with other New Deal legislation, it raised wages for most workers, reduced their hours, abolished child labor, and enacted provisions to make the workplace safe. The Fair Labor Standards Act of 1938 (Wages and Hours Act) established a forty-cent-an-hour minimum wage and a forty-hour workweek for more than 25 million workers engaged in interstate commerce.

Throughout the Industrial Revolution, workers had been clubbed, jailed, beaten, and shot when fighting for the right to have unions—and they got that right in Section 7(a) of the National Industrial Recovery Act. The crucial passage read, "Employees shall have the right to organize and bargain collectively, through representatives of their own choosing, and shall be free from the interference, restraint, or coercion of employers of labor . . ." The National Labor Relations Act of 1935 (the Wagner Act) and the Taft-Hartley Act of 1947 also granted workers the right to have unions. After seventy years of struggle, the sons, daughters, grandsons, and granddaughters of the new immigrants had won what Annie Clemenc had fought so hard to get: equal rights for workers.

The men, women, and children who made these changes possible had the courage to stand up for what they believed was right, and history proved them to be right. They made America rich and powerful. They made America a better place to live and work. This was their legacy, and the legacy of Big Annie of Calumet.

Afterword

With the end of the Michigan copper strike of 1913, prosperity returned to Calumet. There was an increased demand for copper during World War I, which broke out in 1914. But by 1921 an oversupply of copper on the world market caused the Calumet and Hecla Mining Company to close its Michigan operations for almost a year. The company reopened at 50 percent capacity, but copper prices continued to fall during the Depression and through World War II. After years of decline, in 1968 the company closed its last mine in Copper Country. Miners won the right to a union in 1943 when C & H recognized the Western Federation of Miners.

Annie and Joseph Clemenc were divorced, after which Annie moved to Chicago and married Frank Shavs in 1914. At the age of twenty-six, she gave birth to her only child, Darwina, who grew up to be a tall, beautiful woman, bearing a close resemblance to her mother. Frank continued to work as a reporter. During the 1920s and 1930s, while raising Darwina, Annie worked sixteen hours a day at two jobs at different hat-making companies. Her parents moved to Detroit, where they found employment in the automotive industry, as did Joe Clemenc. In midlife Annie experienced more adversity when Darwina lost her left arm in an auto accident. Little is known about Annie's later life, except that Frank became a drunkard and a wife-beater. Annie Clemenc died of cancer in 1956 at the age of sixty-eight.

All but forgotten in history, Annie's story was discovered in the 1970s and recalled in newspapers and magazines. The Italian Hall tragedy was the subject of the play *Mother Lode*, which opened in Detroit in 1980; earlier, Woody Guthrie had immortalized the tragedy in a song, "The 1913 Massacre." Also in 1980, the United States Congress passed a resolution recognizing "the lasting contribution made by remarkable women such as Annie Clemenc," and the Michigan Women's Studies Association honored Annie's memory by commissioning a portrait of Big Annie holding her flag. The portrait was hung in the state capitol. Annie was the first person to be nominated to the Michigan Women's Hall of Fame, and June 17, 1980, was declared Annie Clemenc Day in Michigan. In designating a day for Big Annie, Michigan governor William G. Milliken read a proclamation, which said, in part:

> Annie Clemenc, a long-forgotten leader in the struggle for workers' rights, only recently has been restored to her rightful place on the stage of Michigan history.
>
> This courageous woman stood up to the sabers and bayonets of the cavalry, the economic might of the mine owners, and the scorn of those who insisted her place was in the home.
>
> She became a leading figure in the Upper Peninsula's

historic copper strike of 1913. Recognizing that the struggle for fair treatment for any one person affects the rights of all, she organized the Women's Alliance and marched almost daily—flag in hand—at the head of the demonstrations of mineworkers.

Michigan is now honoring this woman who has come to symbolize courage and resolve in defense of what is right.

Four years later, in October 1984, the long-abandoned Italian Hall was demolished as a safety hazard. Its still-usable bricks were sold for twenty dollars a truckload. Currently fewer than 900 people live in Calumet.

Markers that stand today in Calumet memorializing Big Annie and the Italian Hall tragedy.

Bibliographic Note

Information concerning the copper industry in Michigan, the strike, and the Italian Hall tragedy came from the following primary sources: "Copper-Mine Owners' Side," *Outlook* (February 21, 1914), 397–400; John H. Foster, "Life in the Copper Mines of Lake Superior," *Michigan Pioneer Collection* (1887), 175–86; P. B. McDonald, "Michigan Copper Mines," *Outlook* (February 7, 1914), 297–98; Peter MacFarlane, "The Issues at Calumet," *Collier's* (February 7, 1914), 5; Leslie H. Marcy, "Calumet," *International Socialist Review* (February 1914), 452–61; "Michigan Copper Strike," *Outlook* (January 31, 1914), 237–39; "Michigan Press and the Copper War," *Literary Digest* (January 10, 1914), 47–9; F. W. Taussig, "Copper Strike and Copper Dividends," *Survey* (February 14, 1914), 612–13; Graham R. Taylor, "The Clash in the Copper Country: The First Big Strike in Fifty Years in the Industrial Backwoods of Upper Michigan," *Survey* (November 1, 1913), 127–35; Graham R. Taylor, "Moyer's Story of Why He Left Copper Country," *Survey* (January 10, 1914), 433–55; and Inis Weed, "The Reasons Why the Copper Miners Struck," *Outlook* (January 31, 1914), 247–51.

Annie related her role in the strike in "A Woman's Story," *Miner's Bulletin* (October 2, 1913) and in *Miners' Magazine* (October 23, 1913), 4–5. The record of her arrest when she served ten days in jail was listed People v. Annie Clements [*sic*], Circuit Court, Houghton County Courthouse, File No. 4276.

Conditions in the mines and violence associated with the strike were the subjects of several congressional investigations: U.S. Congress, *Congressional Record*, 63d Cong., lst sess., 1913, 50, p. 6, and 2d sess., 1914, 51, ps. 1, 2, and 3; U.S. Congress, House Committee on Mines and Mining, *Conditions in Copper Mines of Michigan: Hearings before subcommittee pursuant to H.R. 387*, 63d Cong., 2d sess., 1914, 7 ps.; U.S. Congress Committee on Rules, *Industrial Disputes in Colorado and Michigan. Hearings before the Committee on Rules on Resolutions 290 and 313*,

December 10 and 17, 1913, 63d Cong., 2d sess; and U.S. Department of Labor, Bureau of Labor Statistics, *Michigan Copper Strike*, Bulletin No. 139, Washington, 1914, originally printed as S. Doc. 381, Washington, 1914.

The most useful secondary sources were Clarence A. Andrews, "'Big Annie' and the 1913 Michigan Strike," *Michigan History* (Spring 1973), 53–68; William Beck, "Law and Order During the 1913 Copper Strike," *Michigan History* (Winter 1970), 275–92; Virginia L. Burns, *Tall Annie* (Enterprise Press: Haslett, Michigan, 1987); William B. Gates, *Michigan Copper and Boston Dollars: An Economic History of the Michigan Copper Mining Industry*, (1951, Reprint, New York: Russell & Russell, 1969); Andrew S. Lawton, "The Michigan Copper Strike of 1913–14: A Case Study of Industrial Violence During the Age of Reform," Master's thesis, University of Wisconsin, August 1975; William A. Sullivan, "The 1913 Revolt of the Michigan Copper Miners," *Michigan History* (September 1959), 294–314; Arthur W. Thurner, "Charles H. Moyer and the Michigan Copper Strike, 1913–1914," *Michigan Historical Review* (Fall 1992), 1–19; Thurner, *Rebels on the Range: The Michigan Copper Strike of 1913–1914* (Lake Linden, Michigan: John H. Foster Press, 1984); and Michael Wendland, "The Calumet Tragedy," *American Heritage* (April–May 1986), 38–48.

Information on the Industrial Revolution (Chapter 1) came from Thomas R. Brooks, *Toil and Trouble: A History of American Labor* (New York: Dell Publishing Co., 1964); Victor S. Clark, *History of Manufacturers in the United States, 1860–1914* (New York: McGraw–Hill, 1929, reprint); Thomas Cochran and William Miller, *The Age of Enterprise: A Social History of Industrial America* (New York: Macmillan, 1942); John R. Commons (ed.), *The Documentary History of American Industrial Society* (New York: Russell & Russell, 1958, 10 vols.); Samuel P. Hays, *The Response to Industrialism, 1885–1914* (Chicago: University of Chicago Press, 1957); Richard Hofstadter, *Social Darwinism in American Thought* (Boston: Beacon, 1955); Matthew Josephson, *The Robber Barons: The Great American Capitalists, 1861–1901* (New York: Harcourt, Brace & World, Inc., 1962); Malcolm Keir, *The Epic of Industry* (New Haven: Yale University Press, 1926); Edwin C. Kirkland, *Industry Comes of Age: Business, Labor, and Public Policy, 1860–1897* (New York: Holt, Rinehart and Winston, 1961); and Milton Meltzer, *Bread and Roses: The Struggle of American Labor, 1865–1915* (New York: Alfred A. Knopf, 1967).

Information on changes in the law for workers (Chapter 9) came from Irving Bernstein, *The Lean Years: A History of the American Worker, 1920–1933* (New York: Houghton Mifflin Company, 1960); William E. Leuchtenburg, *Franklin D. Roosevelt and the New Deal* (New York: Harper & Row, 1963); and M. B. Schnapper, *American Labor: A Pictorial Social History* (Washington, D.C.: Public Affairs Press, 1972). Some quotations were edited for clarity.

The following individuals were helpful in locating photos and source materials relating to Annie and the strike: Gladys Beckwith, Executive Director, Michigan Women's Historical Center and Hall of Fame; Michael Aubin, Calumet Public Library; and Michael Waldo and Cheryl Rodda, Michigan Technological University Archives and Copper Country Historical Collections, Michigan Technological University, Houghton, Michigan. David Self provided criticism of the manuscript. David and Liz Keranen, longtime dinner companions and residents of the Keweenaw Peninsula whose Finnish ancestors date back to the Industrial Revolution, suggested the story and lobbied for its completion.

Index

Picture Credits

JERRY STANLEY was born in Highland Park, Michigan, in 1941. He received a master's degree and Ph.D. from the University of Arizona. He is now professor of history at California State University at Bakersfield, where he teaches courses on the American West, the American Indian, and California history.

Mr. Stanley is the author of numerous articles for both scholarly journals and popular magazines. His first book, *Children of the Dust Bowl: The True Story of the School at Weedpatch Camp* (1992), was named a Notable Book for Children by the American Library Association and received several distinguished children's books awards, including the Orbis Pictus Award, the California Library Association's John and Patricia Beatty Award, and the Virginia Library Association's Jefferson Cup. His second book, *I Am an American: A True Story of Japanese Internment* (1994), was also named an American Library Association Notable Book for Children.

Among Mr. Stanley's hobbies are bowling, racquetball, fishing, drumming, and writing humor. He lives with his wife, Dorothy, in Bakersfield, California.